ANIMALS *in* DANGER

Giant Panda

Rod Theodorou

Heinemann Library
Chicago, Illinois

Designed by Ron Kamen
Illustrations by Dewi Morris/Robert Sydenham
Originated by Ambassador Litho
Printed by South China Printing in Hong Kong / China
05 04 03 02 01
10 9 8 7 6 5 4 3 2 1

Library of Congress Cataloging-in-Publication Data
Theodorou, Rod.
        Giant panda / Rod Theodorou.
                p. cm. – (Animals in danger)
        Includes bibliographical references (p.).
        Summary: Describes the habitat, behavior, and endangered status of giant pandas and suggests ways to help save them from extinction.
        ISBN 1-57572-264-X (library)
        1. Giant panda—Juvenile literature. [1. Giant panda. 2. Pandas. 3. Endangered species.]
I. Title.

QL737.C214 T44 2000
599.789—dc21

                                                              00-026774

Acknowledgments
The author and publishers are grateful to the following for permission to reproduce copyright material:
Ardea London/ Jean-Paul Ferrero, p. 11, Ardea London/ Adrian Warren, p. 18; BBC Natural History Unit/ Lynn M. Stone, pp. 14, 17, BBC Natural History Unit/ Sue Flood, p. 22; FLPA/ Eichhorn Zingel, p. 4, FLPA/ Gerard Lacz, p. 4, FLPA/ B. Lea & Dembinsky, p. 7, FLPA/ Fritz Polking, p. 9, FLPA/ E. & D. Hosking pp. 12, 27, FLPA/ Leeson Sunset p.13; Holt Studios/ Nigel Cattlin, p. 25; Mike Johnson, p. 4; NHPA/ Henry Ausloos, p. 23, NHPA/ Andy Rouse p. 26; Oxford Scientific Films/ Bates, p. 20; WWF Photolibrary/ Susan A. Mainka, p. 15, WWF Photolibrary/ G. Schaller, p. 19. WWF Photolibrary/ Littlehales p. 5, WWF Photolibrary/ Jim Tuten, p.8, WWF Photolibrary/ Keren Su p.16, WWF Photolibrary/ Ralph R. Reinhold; Still Pictures/ Julio Etchart p. 6, p.24

Cover photograph reproduced with permission of Oxford Scientific Films.
Special thanks to Henning Dräger for his comments in the preparation of this book.

Every effort has been made to contact copyright holders of any material reproduced in this book. Any omissions will be rectified in subsequent printings if notice is given to the publisher.

Some words are shown in bold, **like this.** You can find out what they mean by looking in the glossary.

Contents

Animals in Danger

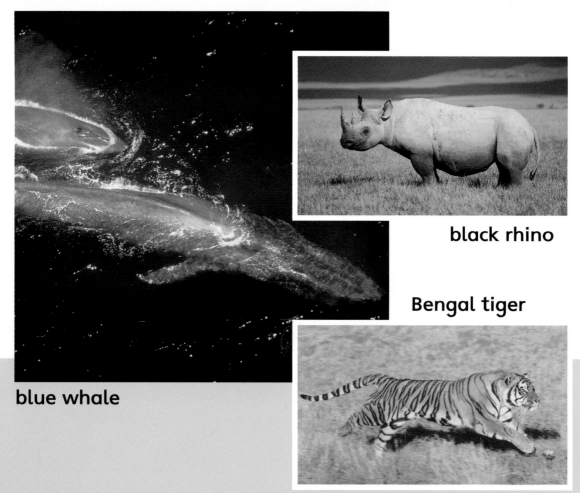

black rhino

Bengal tiger

blue whale

All over the world, more than 10,000 animal **species** are in danger. Some are in danger because their homes are being destroyed. Many are in danger from people hunting them.

4

This book is about giant pandas and why they are **endangered**. Unless people learn to **protect** them, they will become **extinct**. We will only be able to find out about them from books like this.

What are Giant Pandas?

Giant pandas are large **mammals**. They live in the mountains of China, where there are lots of the plants they like to eat. Pandas are very important to the people of China.

For a long time, scientists thought giant pandas were part of the bear family. Now scientists think pandas have their own family, which is closer to **raccoons** than bears.

What Do Giant Pandas Look Like?

Giant pandas look like bears. The fur on their ears, legs, shoulders, and around their eyes is black. The rest of the fur on the panda is white.

Giant pandas can see well. They have strong jaws and teeth for chewing tough food. They have special thumbs to help them hold their food.

Where Do Giant Pandas Live?

CHINA

Key: ▨ where giant pandas live

Giant pandas live only in six small areas of China. They live in the mountain areas around the center of the country.

Giant pandas live high up in the mountains, in cool forests full of **bamboo** plants. There are clouds, rain, and mist here throughout the year.

Giant pandas eat **bamboo** plants. They eat the woody, tough stem and the roots, but they like the green leaves best.

12

Bamboo is not very **nutritious**. Giant pandas have to eat for 10 to 16 hours a day to stay strong and healthy.

Giant Panda Babies

Giant pandas are very shy, and they like to live on their own most of the time. The **males** and **females** only meet in late spring or early summer to **mate**.

Three to five months later the female gives birth to one or two babies, in a **den** in the ground. The babies are called **cubs**. If there are two cubs, only the stronger cub lives to be fully grown.

Caring for the Cub

A newborn giant panda cub is very small and helpless. It cannot see, and it has very little fur. The cub drinks its mother's milk for about six months.

The cub grows slowly. It can move around by itself after three months. After about a year it will go to live on its own. Giant pandas live between 17 and 20 years in the wild.

The giant panda has a special bone on each of its front paws. It uses this bone like a thumb to hold the **bamboo** as it eats.

18

The giant panda is an **omnivore**. It used to eat meat, but a long time ago it changed to mostly eating plants. Sometimes giant pandas also eat small **mammals**, fish, and birds.

How Many Giant Pandas Are There?

One hundred years ago there were large numbers of giant pandas in China. Now there are less than 800 of them in the wild. They are **protected** by **law**.

Nowadays most of the giant pandas live in 13 special **protected** areas in China, called **reserves**. The pandas can live safely in the reserves because people cannot hunt them there.

Why IS the Giant Panda in Danger?

Giant pandas are in danger because of people. They can get caught in traps people set to catch other animals, like deer and black bears.

Hunters in China try to kill pandas to sell their fur for coats. If the hunters are caught they face being punished with the **death penalty**.

Giant pandas are in danger because their **habitat** is being destroyed. Forest areas are being cut down to make room for homes and factories. The trees are sold as wood for making buildings and furniture.

24

Sometimes the **bamboo** plants that the giant pandas eat come into flower. The pandas cannot eat the plants when they have flowers. They have to move and find food, or they will starve.

How is the Giant Panda Being Helped?

Conservation groups work to protect the pandas in the **reserves**. Sometimes the conservation workers care for and raise baby pandas if the mother cannot.

The conservation groups also work to stop people from hunting giant pandas or catching them in traps. Some pandas **mate** and have babies in zoos. The babies are then set free to live in the wild.

27

Giant Panda Fact File

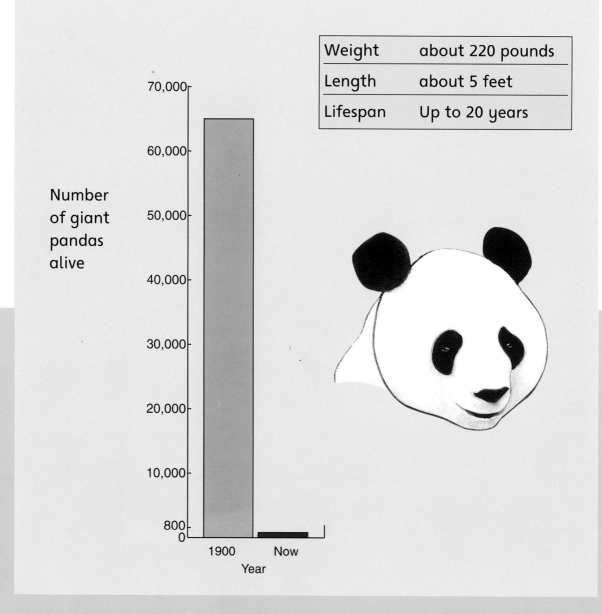

Weight	about 220 pounds
Length	about 5 feet
Lifespan	Up to 20 years

Number of giant pandas alive

70,000
60,000
50,000
40,000
30,000
20,000
10,000
800
0

1900   Now

Year

World Danger Table

	Number that may have been alive 100 years ago	Number that may be alive today
Bengal tiger	100,000	4,500
Blue whale	335,000	4,000
Black rhino	1,000,000	2,000
Mountain gorilla	85,000	500
Florida manatee	75,000	2,000

There are thousands of other animals in the world that are in danger of becoming **extinct**. This table shows some of these animals.

How Can You Help The Giant Panda?

If you and your friends raise money for the giant pandas, you can send it to these organizations. They take the money and use it to pay conservation workers, and to buy food and tools to help save the giant panda.

Defenders of Wildlife
1101 Fourteenth Street, N.W. #1400
Washington, DC 20005

World Wildlife Fund
1250 Twenty-fourth Street
P.O. Box 97180
Washington, DC 20037

More Books to Read

Fichter, George S. *Endangered Animals.* New York, N.Y.: Golden Books Publishing Company, 1995.

Tracqui, Valerie, and BIOS Agency Staff. *The Panda: Wild about Bamboo.* Watertown, Mass: Charlesbridge Publishing, Inc., 1999.

Wexo, John B. *Giant Pandas.* Poway, Cal.: Wildlife Education, Ltd., 1997.

Glossary

bamboo	type of plant with long stems and green leaves
conservation	looking after things, especially if they are in danger
death penalty	when a person is killed as a punishment for doing something wrong
den	place where wild animals live or hide
endangered	group of animals that is dying out, so there are few left
extinct	group of animals that has completely died out and can never live again
female	girl or woman
habitat	home or place where something lives
law	rule or something you have to do
male	boy or man
mammal	warm-blooded animals, like humans, that feed their young on their mother's milk
mate	when a male animal and a female animal come together to make baby animals
nutritious	when a food is healthy and good for you
omnivore	animal that eats both plants and animals
protected	kept safe
raccoon	small animal that has a bushy tail with black and white rings
reserve	large area where animals are looked after by guards
species	group of living things that are very similar

31

Index